Value Meals

on the Volga

Sharing our Heritage with a New Generation

Family Meal Traditions from Mariental, Russia

Anna Dalhaimer Bartkowski

Infinite Adventure Publishing

Value Meals on the Volga: Sharing our Heritage with a New
Generation. Eating Traditions from Mariental, Russia
Copyright@2020 Anna Dalhaimer Bartkowski
3rd Edition

Bartkowski, Anna Dalhaimer
        Value Meals on the Volga: Sharing our Heritage with a New
        Generation. Family Meal Traditions from Mariental, Russia.
        Germans from Russia.

Printed in the United States of America
13 Digit ISBN 978-0-9790720-6-2
10 Digit ISBN 0-9790720-6-9
Library of Congress Control Number: 2020910409

Infinite Adventure Publishing, Chandler, Arizona

This book is intended to provide information regarding the culture
and traditions of Germans from Russia. The book is sold with the
understanding that the author and publisher are not engaged in
rendering nutritional advice or other professional services by
publishing this book. If professional or expert advice is required, it
should be sought. The author and publisher specifically disclaim
any liability, loss, or risk that is incurred as a consequence, directly
or indirectly, of the use and application of any of the contents of this
work. While every attempt is made to provide accurate information,
the book is not guaranteed to be free of errors or omissions. Web
sites and products change therefore it can be expected that not all
suggested sites or products would be accessible or available over
time.

This book is dedicated to my mother, Doris Ann Herzog Dalhaimer, and my paternal grandmother, Clementine Herrmann Dalhaimer Bauer. Without their patient guidance to the next generation, these recipes would have been lost and the family traditions never recorded.

Value Meals on the Volga

Table of Contents

Value Meals on the Volga

Introduction

How will your grandchildren remember you?

Will they have heard your stories often enough to repeat your anecdotes to their children? Will your grandchildren know about their ethnic heritage? The purpose of this book is to show you how you can ensure your stories and heritage live forever in the hearts of your family.

Using tried and true family recipes and stories straight from the heart of the German-Russian village of Mariental, Russia, you can build an unbreakable bond with your children, grandchildren, or great grandchildren. All you need is your kitchen and a few hours of time. These recipes guide you with clear directions and step-by-step photos so whether you are a gourmet chef or a novice cook, you can make delectable delights in your kitchen. And, more than just creating wonderful food, these recipes and family histories will inspire you to share memories of your parents and grandparents no matter what your ancestry is. For me, it means to share the essence of the German-Russian consciousness that today's generation can barely fathom.

German-Russian cooking traditions have been passed from generation to generation and my ancestors in Mariental on the Volga are no exception. Mariental, a small village on the wiesenseite (meadowland) of the Volga River, is where my paternal grandparents, Johannes Thalheimer and Clementine Herrmann, were born, raised, and married. It is a reasonable assumption that

Johannes was a descendent of Mariental founding father, Christopher Thalheimer, and Clementine was a descendent of Nikolaus Herrmann. The list of founding fathers supports my grandmother's stories that both families were among the original Mariental settlers.

After immigrating to the United States not once, but twice, Clementine settled in Sheboygan, Wisconsin for the remainder of her life. Feeding all five of her children was no easy task on a peasant's income. My grandmother learned her cooking skills from her mother, Barbara Spies Herrmann. This knowledge would serve Clementine well. Vegetables and meats were real treats and, unfortunately, were not the staples of the household. The lack of meat certainly made Catholic fasting, with no meat on Fridays, much easier to bear.

When my mother, Doris Herzog, married my father, Joseph Dalhaimer, she did not have much experience cooking the meals to which my father was accustomed. Doris' mother, Sophie, was born in Reinwald, Russia, and immigrated to the United States as a young girl. Sophie raised eight children, and as the youngest child, my mother remembers chickens in the backyard when she grew up on Superior Avenue in Sheboygan. When my daughter, Becky, questioned my mother about her recollections of life during the Great Depression, Becky wrote:

All families had a garden in their backyard in which they grew onions, tomatoes, potatoes, lettuce, carrots, radishes, and cabbage. These were considered the substantial foods upon which people survived. Doris' family also had a plum tree, and different fruit bushes were also common—particularly raspberry bushes. Food was, for the most part, completely a product of her family members' labor. Her mother (Sophie) tended the garden, and her father (Fred) raised rabbits in a shed behind their home and would kill them so that the family could eat meat for Sunday dinner. Anytime Sophie bought chicken for a meal, her daughters would pluck the feathers, and Sophie would clean out the chicken and prepare the meat. Occasionally, the chicken would still have an egg, making the purchase a better investment. Doris' family ate only homemade bread, which was a unique quality because when she brought her lunch to school the other children had store-bought bread. Sophie normally made dough-based meals, recipes native to Russia, her birthplace.

So, while Doris was aware of her mother's cooking and ate many homegrown foods during the Depression, it was unnecessary for her to learn to cook at that time in her life.

None of my father's favorite recipes were written or recorded anywhere to Doris' knowledge. The recipes were stored in my grandmother Clementine's memory. To learn my father's favorite meals, Doris asked her new mother-in-law for help.

Clementine was willing to share her expertise by showing Doris how to prepare these meals. When my grandmother demonstrated cooking to my mother, Clementine simply said, "Put in about this much flour... add about that much sugar," etc. My mother knew there was no way she could duplicate the exact amounts visually, so she diligently watched my grandmother scoop ingredients. Then Doris measured every item, and painstakingly recorded the ingredients and amounts for each recipe. My mother watched and followed this pattern until she perfected each meal. In this way my grandmother passed her cooking skills on to my mother.

In this book, I have expanded my mother's written notes of each recipe and provided detailed instructions with full color photographs to help every cook envision the process and continue to pass on these traditions to a new generation.

While these recipes have nothing on the Food Network or Julia Child, they do document traditions in the Thalheimer and Herrmann family, undoubtedly learned and passed through many generations. These meals were used in times of plenty and in times of hardship. German-Russian cooks created value out of every meal. These meals fed hungry workers so they would have full stomachs when they went to tend the harvest in the field. The meals took time and effort to make. The original meals were simple, and the traditional recipes are recorded here. To ensure passage and celebration of these recipes for generations to come, some of the basics are enhanced. As my sisters and I continue to make these meals, some modern-day short cuts and a few healthy alternatives have been incorporated so we can continue to enjoy our German-Russian traditions in our busy lives. These alternative recipes are presented adjacent to the original instructions.

In addition to the original and modern recipes, I have included family anecdotes, beverage recommendations and pronunciation guides.

Family anecdotes act as a catalyst to spark your memories. One story leads to another and another. I hope the stories I share trigger your own recollections. The last page of the book includes space for recording your stories as kitchen conversations unfold. Be sure to visit my blog at www.blogspot.valuemeals.com to discover family history updates and to share your family memories.

Beverage recommendations add a full meal dimension to the simple food. My ancestors did not have the means to enjoy fine wines, beer, or other beverages as we can today. In fact, I have heard the phrase that German Russians "did not dine, they ate." I know my grandmother enjoyed a shot of peppermint schnapps when she could, and I believe she would enjoy the adaptations and abundance added to her meals.

All spellings and recipe names are part of our family traditions. Other families may have recipes with similarities or distinct variations: however, these are the ones my family has cherished over the years. For example, Mariental is the accepted spelling of my ancestral village and it is pronounced *Mary en tal*. My grandparents spelled the city as Marienthal and pronounced it as *Marie en thal* with the emphasis on *Marie*. Therefore, I have also included a pronunciation guide with the German-Russian recipe titles. Again, these are the pronunciations my family used.

I sincerely hope these recipes bring back some of your German-Russian or ethnic family memories. And I pray this compilation provides you with future pleasures as these recipes are shared with coming generations. It is in our hands to pass our heritage on to our children and grandchildren. No matter how busy our children's lives are, it behooves us to spend at least a day or two each year to share these skills and create lifetime memories for our grandchildren.

L to R; Clementine Herrmann Dalhaimer Bauer and her granddaughter Anna Dalhaimer Bartkowski

L to R: Anna Dalhaimer Bartkowski and her mother Doris
Herzog Dalhaimer

While our German-Russian ancestors ate these meals frequently, one of the ways we can honor and healthily enjoy our culinary heritage is to incorporate these meals into our holiday traditions. The history of these recipes has been passed from woman to woman, although I encourage you to include boys, girls, teenagers, and young adults in these traditions. Time spent sharing, creating. and bonding in the kitchen is an equal opportunity enjoyment.

The comfort of a warm stove and a great meal provides the best quality time between generations. What memories will you share or create with your next cooking session? Find out in *Value Meals on the Volga* how you can ensure your family traditions live forever by building an unbreakable bond with a new generation now.

Preparation and Planning

The preparation and planning phase of cooking is critical to the success of your project. Here is a checklist to use to be sure you have considered all angles before you embark on your cooking adventure.

1. **What equipment do I need?**

   Rolling pin, clean surfaces, bowls, etc. If it has been some time since your last project, check to make sure all tools are in good working order.

2. **What ingredients do I need?**

   Each recipe is unique, so review the list of ingredients and double-check your pantry.

3. **How much time do I need for the project?**

   A few of the recipes call for preparation one day and cooking the next day. Read the recipe again to make sure your expectations and schedule will fit properly.

4. **What should be worn while cooking?**

   There is a reason many cooks wear aprons. I recommend pulling one out of the drawer, or if it has been several years since you have owned one, you can buy or sew a new one. Aprons are relatively easy to make if you have even basic sewing skills. If you prefer not to use an apron, I recommend some old clothes since the flour may fly during some of the preparation phases.

5. With whom will you be cooking?

I love to cook with my mother, and it is easy since she is an expert on these meals. When I work with my children, I need to do a bit of explaining on the techniques. Children of all ages can help and it is a good idea to plan of time the steps they can do best. Use your judgment based on their age and ability to follow directions. Some children may simply enjoy watching a meal made from scratch!

6. Clean up the little messes as you go along.

When you are done with a utensil, bowl, or dish, rinse it and set it in the dishwasher or deep clean it immediately so the clean-up at the end is not as arduous. This is easy to do since each recipe has some mini breaks. Cooking German-Russian style is not for the faint of heart. It is messy, especially if you turn on the mixer before the beater is placed completely in the bowl. Flour flies as you can see from the picture below, but it created a great memory for my daughter Ashley and me. Can you imagine always

stirring the dough by hand? I, for one, do not have the strength or stamina to do it. I am so grateful for having a hands-free and KitchenAid mixer.

7. Plan for fun!

Plan for fun and enjoy the creative and indulgent experience of genuine German-Russian food. Plan to work safe with all equipment and utensils.

Soups

Green Bean Soup

This soup is my sister Cheryl's favorite German-Russian recipe. I cannot make it without thinking of her. Occasionally, my mother would forego the potatoes in this soup. Green bean soup without potatoes was unacceptable to my sister. My mother recommends 3 potatoes, however, based on your preference, you could use up to six for potato lovers. For green bean lovers, using more green beans, whether canned, fresh, or frozen, is fantastic. This hearty soup is an excellent addition to your Lenten meal schedule or when the cold weather keeps you indoors.

Soup Ingredients
  Water, for boiling, fill 2/3 of 8 qt. pot
  3 potatoes peeled and cut into ½ inch pieces
  2 tablespoons butter
  ½ cup flour
  8 oz. container sour cream
  One 16 oz. can of green beans or fresh green beans

Dumpling Ingredients:
  3 cups flour
  1 tablespoon salt
  2 eggs
  1 ¼ cups water

Heat water and salt in 8-quart pot until boiling. Skin and cut 3 medium size potatoes (white, russet, Idaho, or any variety you enjoy works well) into ½ to one-inch pieces. Add cut potatoes to boiling water. Mix dumpling ingredients in large bowl with a sturdy spoon. Scoop dumpling dough into small tablespoon sizes and drop gently into pot. Add green beans. Boil with potatoes for 15-20

minutes. In separate frying pan, place 2 tablespoons of butter and 1/2 cup flour. Warm this mixture on low heat while stirring occasionally. Heat until the flour browns and butter dissolves. The above photo shows how the flour appears when the butter has separated into small clumps. In the

photograph below, the flour is browned. Some family prefer the broth light, while others prefer the flour be completely blackened. Experiment with it and find your favorite flavor. In my mother's opinion, the flour can never get too black.

Add browned flour to water in pot. Be careful to add the flour slowly as it may spritz out of the soup kettle. Stir until mixture is blended through the water. Add sour cream to thicken the broth. The soup can simmer until you are ready to serve it. Green Bean Soup serves a family of four for at least 2 meals.

Modern, healthy alternatives for Green Bean Soup:

- Substitute fresh or frozen green beans for canned green beans
- Use soy sour cream or light sour cream in lieu of regular sour cream
- Use organic, cage free eggs, eggbeaters, or egg replacers
- Use whole-wheat flour or Hodgson Mill all-purpose unbleached naturally white flour. Visit their web site at http://www.hodgsonmill.com/
- Add pearl onions for a unique twist
- Experiment with seasonings like red pepper or oregano

Beverage Recommendation:

Since my mother's maiden name is Herzog, we like to drink Baron Herzog Chardonnay or Shiraz with our soup if we are in the mood for wine. This is a hearty soup; therefore, a nice mug of beer is another great alternative. I recommend Spaten from Munich or a domestic Amber Bock.

The only photo of my paternal great-grandmother,

Barbara Spies Herrmann.

Rice Glacyer Soup
(pronounced Rice Glacier Soup)

The bread is the feature in this fantastic soup also known as Bread Ball Soup. I have often asked my mother what the purpose is of separating the whites and the crusts of the bread. The answer remains unknown; however, one version concludes that the separation and re-combining adds texture to the bread ball. My mother prefers the bread loaf sit out a day or two before separating the whites and crusts. She also recommends the separated whites and crusts rest for 24 hours before combining.

Soup bones used to be free for the asking in butcher or grocery stores when I was a young girl. Today it is rare to see these bones available and, if found, the price is considerably more than when my grandmother made this recipe. I like to opt for the vegetable broth since my daughters do not eat meat, chicken, pork, or fish.

Ingredients:

One loaf of white bread (2-3 days old)	1 tablespoon salt
Beef roast with bone or soup bones	4 eggs
¼ lb. melted butter	1 cup cooked rice

A day before you plan to serve the soup, break up bread into two separate bowls of white and crusts. Let sit uncovered for 24 hours.

Whites and crusts of bread are separated into two bowls

The next day, boil beef roast or soup bones in salted water in an 8-quart pot. While the water is starting to boil, place the whites and crusts of bread into one bowl, add 4 eggs and ¼ lb. melted butter and mix. Shape bread mixture into small one-inch balls.

Remove bone from boiling water. Add bread balls to boiling water and boil until the balls rise to the top of the kettle. Add 1 cup cooked rice to soup

Beef can remain in soup or be removed as preferred. If you enjoy eating beef on the side, this mustard sauce is a great treat for dipping.

Mustard Sauce for Beef

Combine one teaspoon dry mustard, two teaspoons sugar and a little broth.

Modern, healthy alternatives for Rice Glaceyer Soup:

- Use organic, cage free eggs, eggbeaters, or egg replacers
- Use whole wheat, multi-grain, or whole grain white bread for bread balls
- Use brown rice or couscous instead of white rice
- Use beef broth, chicken broth, or vegetable broth in lieu of beef or soup bones
- Use Smart Balance instead of butter
- Pouring a bit of beer in the broth adds a nice German touch.

Rice Glaceyer soup ready to enjoy

Beverage Recommendation:

Bitburger or Spaten beers are good choices with this soup. As an after-dinner drink/dessert, my mother and I enjoy a glass of Carolan's Irish Crème on ice.

Engagement photo of Johannes Thalheimer and Clementine Herrmann. This photo was taken in Mariental, Russia about 1912.

Main
Dishes

Fleisch & Kraut Bierok

(Pronounced Fleisch and Kraut Bier Rock or Bar Uck, Rhymes with Yuck)

This is a great meal for any day of the week. At the Dalhaimer house, we typically ate bierok for our Sunday dinner. And, by dinner, I mean the main meal of the day, which was served at 12 noon. As my daughter Becky translates, "Dinner was lunch and supper was dinner." Although the traditional method calls for ground beef, bierok makes an excellent vegetarian meal.

Ingredients:

4 cups of water
One onion, diced
½ lb. ground beef, cooked
Salt and pepper to taste
1 head cabbage
¼ cup butter or vegetable oil
Original Bread mixture or use Pillsbury Hot Roll Mix-requires 1 cup hot water, 2 tablespoons softened butter or margarine, and 1 egg

Grease a 9x13 inch-baking pan with vegetable oil or spray with canola, olive, or vegetable oil. Preheat oven to 350° F.

Heat 4 cups of salted water in large kettle to boiling. While water is heating, dice the onion. Place ground beef and half of the diced onion in frying pan and heat thoroughly until meat is completely cooked. Add salt and pepper for seasoning.

Cut cabbage into slivers. Add the cabbage and the remainder of the diced onion to boiling water. Add salt and pepper to taste. Boil until cabbage is soft and tender.

While cabbage and ground beef cook, start to prepare the dough. Unfortunately, the original bread mixture recipe has been lost however we have successfully substituted Pillsbury's Hot Roll Mix for years. Follow the Hot Roll directions for mixing. Knead dough for 5 minutes until smooth. Let dough rest for 5 minutes.

Continue to check the meat and cabbage. When cabbage is tender, drain the water from the cabbage pot using a sieve placed in your kitchen sink. Set cabbage aside. Reduce heat on meat as needed.

After roll mix has rested, cut the dough into 4 equal parts. Use rolling pin to roll one of the parts of the dough into the shape of a rectangle until approximately ¼ inch thick. Add flour or oil as needed if the dough is sticky. Cut the rolled dough into four squares.

Pinch the ends of the dough together to create the square filled with cabbage, meat, or both.

Scoop the cabbage or meat mixture with a tablespoon and place the mixture on the center of one of the squares. Or combine the cabbage and meat mixtures together and then place onto the center of each of the squares. With floured fingers, pinch together two opposite ends of the square and then bring the remaining two ends together. Gently pinch the open edges together until the square dough cover holds the mixture inside.

Above: one quarter of the dough is rolled flat then cut in quarters with boiled cabbage mixture scooped on the top. The portion in the lower right-hand corner has already been pinched together.

Place each square into the baking pan with pinched edges down. Repeat the process with remaining 3 parts of the dough. When all the squares are in the baking pan, brush with melted butter or oil if desired. Cover with kitchen cloth and let bierok rise for 20-30 minutes. Bake at 350 degrees for 20-25 minutes. Meal serves family of four for two meals.

These squares are not perfectly shaped; however, it was the first time my daughter, Ashley, tried to prepare this meal and she did a fabulous job. With practice, the squares will be more evenly shaped, however the shape of the square does not affect the great taste of the meal. Her meal was fantastic!

Bierok is ready to eat!

Modern, healthy alternatives for Fleisch & Kraut Bierok:
- Use ground turkey or soy beef instead of ground beef
- Use sea salt, seasoning salt, or red pepper for variety
- For the inside mixture, some individuals enjoy meat only, some enjoy cabbage only and others prefer to have the meat and cabbage mixed. Experiment and find out your favorite flavor option. The cabbage only version is great for a vegetarian meal
- Use organic, cage free eggs, eggbeaters, or egg replacers

Beverage Recommendation:

Baron Herzog, Yarden or Klinker Brick wines are great additions to this meal.

The Saw

This saw belonged to my grandfather, Johannes Thalheimer, whose name was recorded as Dalhaimer when he entered the United States. It is the only possession passed to his son, Joseph.

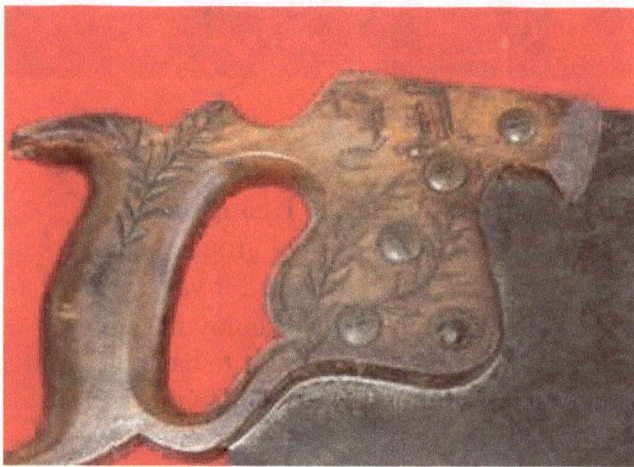

What is of interest is the beautiful carving on the handle. In addition to what appears to be the manufacturer's design, his initials J.D. are engraved at the top. The name Mariental, his birthplace in Russia, was carved directly on the handle nearly worn away from use and only visible under close examination.

The story as told by my grandmother Clementine to my father was that Johannes bought the saw in the United States. He returned to Mariental when my grandmother was extremely homesick. In Mariental, he had the carvings added to the saw. Within a short time, they again immigrated to the United States, taking the saw with him for the return journey. My father gave the saw to me in the 1980s.

The Picture Hidden in the Prayer Book

Clementine Herrmann Thalheimer always kept this picture in her German prayer book. The book, "Die Freude in Gott," was given to my father after Clementine's death. My father gave it to me in the 1980's when I began my genealogical search. The book is dated 1897.

My father told me the young girl in the picture was Clementine's daughter Rosie. According to the family Bible records, Rosie was born February 15, 1918. Rosie was the first child of Clementine and Johannes to live past infancy. Clementine adored and terribly missed Rosie when she died in 1921.

Clementine held Rosie's memory close with this picture. After the first edition of this book was published, my cousin Janet Peaslee told me the girl in the picture was her mother, Tinie Dalhaimer Fromm. Which story is correct? It is difficult to know. The scratches on the photo to the right of Clementine's head add another mystery to this intriguing picture.

Sour Cream Mauldasha aka Ra Maultaschen
(pronounced sour cream mull da sha or ra mull da sha)

My mother always made this dish in a brown pan. My sister Joan and I could not pronounce the name of the meal, so for years, we simply called it "the stuff in the brown pan." This "stuff" is Joan's favorite German-Russian dish. We traditionally enjoyed this meal on Friday nights.

Ingredients:

3 cups flour
1 tablespoon salt
½ tablespoon sugar
1 teaspoon baking powder
2 eggs

1 ½ cups water
3 tablespoons butter
4 cups milk
8 oz. sour cream

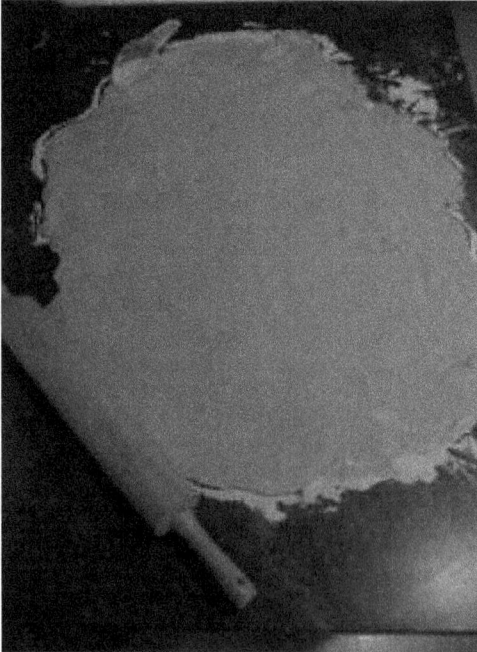

Preheat oven to 450 ° F. Mix flour, salt, sugar, baking powder and eggs in large bowl. Add 1½ cups of water. Mix until all ingredients form dough. Knead the dough until smooth.

Add flour if necessary, to make a stiff but malleable dough. Use rolling pin to spread out thinly, approximately ¼ inch thick on a floured board.

Set 13x9x2 inch pan with 3 tablespoons of butter in it over a burner. Heat butter on low until melted. Warm 4 cups milk on low heat on stovetop and set aside.

Spread sour cream over the flattened dough just like you would spread frosting on a cake.

Rolled Dough with sour cream spread over it.

Cut the dough with a sharp knife into square/rectangular pieces. Roll up each piece lengthwise into a circular tube, like a Swiss cake roll. Set each tube into the pan with the melted butter. Arrange in pan as it fits best. Pour warm milk over rolls.

Bake in 450° oven for approximately 30 minutes. Lower oven temperature after milk boils. Meal serves family of four for two meals. Leftovers can be cut up and re-heated in frying pan or microwave.

Mauldasha fresh out of the oven.

Modern, healthy alternatives for Sour Cream Mauldasha:

- Use skim milk or soy milk instead of regular milk
- Use soy sour cream or light sour cream in lieu of regular sour cream
- Use Smart Balance in place of butter
- Use whole wheat flour, organic flour, or all-purpose unbleached naturally white flour
- Use organic, cage free eggs, eggbeaters, or egg replacers

Beverage Recommendation:

I prefer to drink a German Riesling white wine with this meal. Two good choices are Pacific Rim Riesling or Fetzer Vineyards.

Family Portrait Circa 1931

Family Photo front row left to right, my father Joseph Dalhaimer, Clementine Herrmann Dalhaimer Bauer, Fred Bauer, Gottlieb Bauer, and John Dalhaimer. Back row left to right Tinie Dalhaimer Fromm and Zeaman Dalhaimer.

My father recalled he got a nosebleed shortly before this photo session and lived to regret it when his mother saw the blood on his new suit. The source of his bloody nose was his brother, John. The stains are visible on his right upper sleeve.

Gottlieb Bauer was the only father my Dad ever knew. Gottlieb was from Schäffer, Russia and we knew very little of his family history. According to his death certificate, his parents were Phillip and Anna Elizabeth Bauer. My former classmate, Carol Bauer Wheeler, has shared many more details on his family tree.

<u>Cottage Cheese Mauldasha</u>
(Pronounced Cottage cheese mull da sha)

When my mother and I made our latest batch of cottage cheese mauldasha, she shared with me a Christmas Day tradition of the Herzog children. No matter how freezing cold, windy, snowy, or icy the weather was on December 25th in Sheboygan, Wisconsin, her parents would send all the children to her grandfather's house. The children walked from 17th & Superior Ave. to 11th & Erie Ave. Once at her grandfather's house, the children would greet him with "Fröhliche Weihnachten und ein Neues Jahre!" Her grandfather would invite all eight of them inside and give each a shot of port wine. Then, they would head back home in the cold. This tradition was their way of life. It was never considered a hardship, but a treasured memory for my mother. And they really looked forward to the warmth of the port wine.

Doris' grandfather, Phillip Reimer who immigrated from Reinwald, Russia with his wife and three young daughters, was a recognizable figure in the city of Sheboygan because he walked every day of his life. Of course, during his lifetime, very few families owned cars. My father recognized Philip Reimer due to his walks before my Dad ever met my mother. Philip never wore a heavy overcoat only a suit jacket, and he drank the mineral water from the "bubbler" at Fountain Park on 8th Street every day. He would fill a jug of water and carry it until he returned home. He never drank regular tap water, so in many ways he was ahead of his time.

Perhaps that is why he lived 94 years and was rarely sick a day in his life.

This "bubbler," or water fountain, produced water with "medicinal value." For more details on the mineral water, please see Appendix A. As a child, I ran to the "bubbler" one day, drank it and could hardly believe what I swallowed. My face contorted expressing the shock of tasting saline, mineral water instead of regular tap water. What memories will you share or create with your next cooking session?

Cottage Cheese Filling Ingredients:

16 oz. container of Cottage Cheese	1 tablespoon Salt
1 egg	Breadcrumbs Optional: Raisins

Mix cottage cheese filling ingredients together. Add enough breadcrumbs to reduce moisture of cottage cheese. Stir mixture until it is well blended and cohesive. Set aside.

Dough Ingredients:

3 cups Flour   1 cup water

2 eggs   Melted butter

Bring to a boil a quart of water in a large kettle. While water is boiling, mix dough ingredients together and knead dough until a firm consistency is reached.

Divide dough into three parts. Roll one part of the dough flat to approximately ¼ inch thick with rolling pin. Cut flat dough into 4 inch by 4-inch squares. Scoop a spoonful of the cottage cheese filling and place onto the center of each square.

Stretch the dough as needed to pinch together two opposite ends of square. Then, pull together the two remaining ends and pinch the edges together until the dough securely wraps the filling.

Repeat with the remaining two parts of dough. Place each pillowed square into the boiling water. Cut any leftover dough edges into thin strips approximately ½" wide and add to boiling water. Return water to a boil and cook for 15-20 minutes. Drain. Serve immediately and pour melted butter over dish as desired.

This meal has been my favorite for years. I especially enjoy the leftover strips. As a great leftover meal, the cottage cheese mauldasha can be lightly fried. My most recent tradition is to make this meal on Christmas Eve.

Modern, healthy alternatives for Cottage Cheese Mauldasha:

- Use wheat or multi-grain breadcrumbs
- Use Smart Balance in place of butter
- Use organic, cage free eggs, eggbeaters, or egg replacers
- Use whole wheat flour, organic flour, or all-purpose unbleached naturally white flour
- Instead of making dough, boil lasagna noodles as directed on package. Layer the noodles and cottage cheese filling in a 13x9x2 inch pan. Rotate layers. The last layer must be noodles. Top with melted butter. Bake for 30 minutes in 350° F. oven.

Beverage Recommendation:

On Christmas Eve, my parents and grandmother typically drank old fashioned, whiskey sour or brandy and coke mixed drinks. I discovered any good merlot also works well. Since I am from Wisconsin, a cold mug of Leinenkugel's Beer makes me feel at home no matter where I am. For more details on Leinie, which is brewed in Chippewa Falls, Wisconsin, visit their web site at www.leinie.com/welcome.html.

My mother, Doris Ann Herzog, at her confirmation in 8th grade at Ebenezer Lutheran Grade School in Sheboygan, Wisconsin in 1941. She was fourteen years old. Ebenezer Lutheran was affectionately known as the "German-Russian College."

My maternal grandparents,
Sophie Reimer Herzog and Fred Herzog

Sophie was born in Reinwald, Russia and immigrated to the
United States with her parents and three sisters
when she was 3 years old.
Fred's birthplace according to his death certificate
was also Reinwald, Russia, however through further research
I discovered he was born in the daughter colony of Rosenfeld
am Nachoi. Fred would walk from their home on 17th and
Superior to the bakery on 13th and Superior to buy day-old
items that he would bring back in a gunnysack.
The Herzog family had eight children
for whom to provide.
However, Doris says that they never experienced hunger and
never truly thought about being poor because everyone she
associated with was poor as well.

Dumplings
(Pronounced Dump lings)

This dish is great as a main course or side dish. It is one of the faster recipes, so it works well for weekday dinner, too. While I always enjoyed the melted butter over my dumpling, my Dad really liked topping the dumplings with warm strawberries. Of course, strawberry short cake was his favorite dessert.

My sister Joan skips the first meal serving and goes directly to the leftover version of this meal. In fact, when we made dumplings recently, my mother expected the leftover version; however, we ate the traditional meal first and made the leftover version the next day. The leftover version works well for breakfast, too. Check the leftover instructions after the original recipe.

Ingredients:
4 quarts boiling water
3 cups flour
Melted butter
1 1/4 cups water

1 tablespoon salt
2 eggs
Optional: Strawberries

Place 4 quarts of water into an 8-quart pot and heat. As water heats, mix all ingredients, except strawberries, in a large bowl until it forms cohesive dough.

Use a large tablespoon to scoop spoonfuls of dumplings and place gently into the boiling water. Let the dumplings cook for 15-20 minutes. Drain. Pour melted butter over dumplings. If desired, add warmed strawberries.

Modern, healthy alternatives for Dumplings:

- Use whole wheat flour, organic flour, or all-purpose unbleached naturally white flour
- Use organic, cage free eggs, eggbeaters, or egg replacers
- Use Smart Balance instead of butter

This beautiful hand me down plate was passed from my grandmother to my mother and then to me. On the back of the plate it reads, "Currier & Ives 'The Old Grist Mill' Underglaze Print by Royal, Made in the U.S.A."

Beverage Recommendation:
If you serve the leftover dumplings for breakfast, a good cup of coffee is your best bet. Spaten or Leinenkugel beer is a special treat with this meal for dinner or supper.

Leftover Instructions:

Cut up remaining dumplings into one-inch pieces. Heat oil in frying pan and, when warm, place dumpling pieces in the pan. Let the dumplings warm until slightly brown. Add four to eight eggs to the frying pan. The amount of eggs varies as to how many dumplings are leftover. Experiment with the number to suit your taste and your fondness of eggs. Stir frequently while mixture heats until the eggs reach the consistency of scrambled eggs. Enjoy! For individuals who enjoy Tabasco or ketchup with their eggs, add liberally as desired. Photo below shows leftover dumplings in frying pan.

Microwave option:

Cut up dumplings and place in microwavable dish. Heat in microwave for one minute. Add four to six eggs to the dish. The amount of eggs corresponds to how many dumplings are leftover. Heat again for one minute. Remove dish from microwave and stir. Heat for another two minutes and stir as needed. Heat in one-minute increments until the eggs reach the consistency you desire. Enjoy! For individuals who enjoy Tabasco or ketchup with their eggs, add liberally as desired.

Leftover Dumplings ready to eat

World War II

My Dad's family posed for this picture in the backyard at
1127 St. Clair Avenue in Sheboygan, Wisconsin. From left to right,
Fred Bauer, Joseph Dalhaimer, Clementine Herrmann Dalhaimer
Bauer, Susie Dalhaimer (daughter of Zeaman and Edna), Gottlieb
Bauer and Zeaman Dalhaimer. My dad, Joseph, is in his navy
uniform. His older brother, John, is not in the photograph because
he was already serving in the Marines during World War II. Despite
their German-Russian heritage, the family's patriotism for their new
country was valued. During the war, my grandmother lost touch
with all her family in Mariental. Her letters were never returned nor
reciprocated after the start of the war. Clementine assumed they
were killed or sent to Siberia. She prayed they survived Siberia.

After years of family research, I received an email from Wladimir Herrmann. He asked if I was related to Clementine Herrmann Dalhaimer. Through much online communication, we determined that Wladimir is the grandson of my grandmother's youngest brother, Anton. Their journey from Mariental to Siberia, Kazakhstan, Russia and ultimately Germany could fill another book. I fulfilled a lifelong dream when I traveled to Germany in 2018 and re-united with Herrmann relatives who had been separated for over one hundred years. My sister, Joan, and her husband, John Gamache, traveled with me for the journey of a lifetime. I was delighted to meet Tante Maria, my father's cousin who was born in Mariental and remembers the train ride to Siberia.

Left to right: Wladimir Herrmann, Maria Herrmann Sokolov, Anna Dalhaimer Bartkowski, Maria Herrmann Aab aka Tante Maria, Joan Mary Dalhaimer Gamache.

It was an honor to meet all my newfound cousins who shared a common ancestor, Nickolaus Herrmann, the man who left the area now known as Luxembourg and became an original settler of Mariental. Before Nickolaus and his wife, Magdalena, departed from Stadt Bredimus, they were married at the church shown below, where Wladimir and I stood in their footsteps. Note the year 1754 on the door frame above our heads.

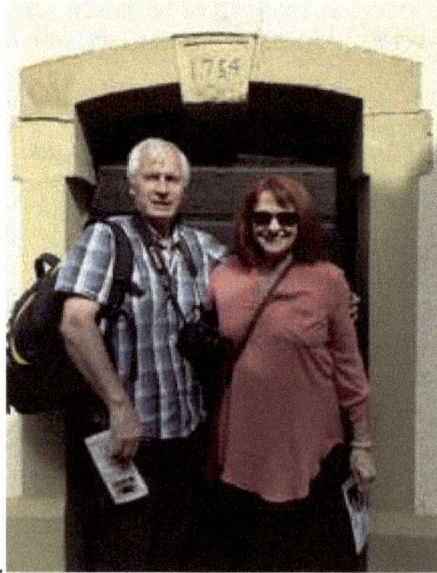

1.

My cousins' hospitality and graciousness in accepting us into their homes was priceless. To travel to Wittlich, Stadt Bredimus and Bitche, France, and other Germanic origin sites, with my cousin, sister and brother-in-law was a dream come true.

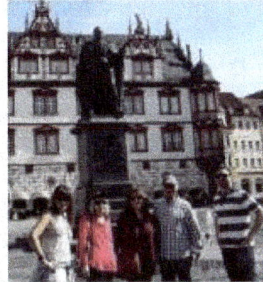

Top left: Back row, Alex Herrmann, Wladimir Herrmann, Fortunada Herrmann, Anna Dalhaimer Bartkowski, Joan and John Gamache. Top right: Natalia Erkenbrecher, Joan Gamache, Anna Dalhaimer Bartkowski, John Gamache Christian Erkenbrecher in town square Coburg.

Middle Left: Wladimir Herrmann and Anna Dalhaimer Bartkowski at Porta Nigra. Middle: Mertes Winery in Wittlich, one of our maternal ancestral villages

Bottom: John Gamache, Joan Dalhaimer Gamache, and Anna Dalhaimer Bartkowski at the Moselle and Saar Rivers Tree Top Village.

I feel fortunate to have such accomplished relatives who have survived through our world's changes. I learned much about love, family and the ties that bind during this adventure.

Wladimir is not only my cousin, he is an expert researcher in Russian, German and English. He crafted his book "Nachkommen von Nikolaus Herrmann aus Luxemburg" in German and Russian after years and years of family tracking. It is the ultimate guide to the Herrmann settlers in Mariental. It was my honor to donate copies to the American Historical Society of Germans from Russia headquarters in Lincoln, Nebraska. I savored the moment when I visited the library in July of 2019 as shown below.

BRODA
(Pronounced Bro da)

Broda is a great Sunday meal. When I was growing up, Sunday meals always worked around the Green Bay Packer schedule. The tradition has continued in my household and we need to plan our meals around Sunday and Monday night games, too.

Pickling spice was a staple in our household, however, not all stores currently offer this spice. For additional information on making your own pickling spice or how to locate it, see Appendix C.

Ingredients:

6 pork chops	Vegetable, safflower, or canola oil
4 quarts of water	2 tablespoons Pickling spice
Bay Leaf	1 medium onion
3 tablespoons butter	Salt

Wash pork chops and place in 8 qt. pot with 4 quarts of water and a bay leaf. Heat to boiling and boil for 15 minutes. While boiling, peel whole potatoes and cut the potatoes in half lengthwise. Place the potatoes round side up on one half of 13x9x2 inch pan.

Melt 3 tablespoons of butter in small pan on stove or microwavable dish in microwave. Mix butter with 3 tablespoons oil and pour over potatoes. Remove pork chops and bay leaf from pot. Place pork chops on the other half of the pan. Distribute the two tablespoons of pickling spice evenly between the two corners of the meat side of the pan. Quarter the onion. Place one quarter of the onion in each of the four corners of the pan.

Add broth from pot to pan to fill approximately up to 5/8 of the height of the pan. Save remaining broth.

Cover only the meat side of the pan with aluminum foil. Bake at 450° F. for one hour. For browner potatoes, adjust the heat to broil for the last 5 minutes. Add extra broth to pan as needed during or after baking.

Broda with potatoes and pork chops before cooking

Broda in the pan with browned and lightly browned potatoes. My father enjoyed the lightly browned potatoes and would mash it with extra broth on his plate. My mother and I preferred the browner, crunchier potatoes.

Modern, healthy alternatives for Broda:

- Use Smart Balance instead of butter and use extra virgin olive oil in place of regular oil

- Use sea salt, seasoning salt, or onion salt in place of regular salt

- Make the meal ahead of time and refrigerate up to eight hours and then bake.

- For vegetarians, make a separate pan of potatoes with the same seasoning. Use a 14 oz. can of vegetable broth instead of broth from the pork chops. See the photos on page 59 for vegetarian broda before and after baking.

Broda is ready to eat.

Beverage Recommendation:

Anything goes. However, I would choose a favorite wine followed by a shot of schnapps after the meal.

Vegetarian broda before baking and ready to eat

Gottlieb and Clementine Bauer standing near the back door of their home on St. Clair Ave. Gottlieb was a meticulous gardener and tended the yard, so the flowers and trees were in perfect condition. Clementine had a kitchen on the main floor of her house; yet she did most of her cooking in the basement kitchen. The table she used to "roll out the dough" was salvaged by my father who scraped years of flour, sugar and sweat off the surface. He refinished the wood beautifully. The table was part of my parent's house on 20th Street for years and it now resides in my sister Joan's house in Eugene, Oregon.

My parents, Joseph, and Doris, walking out the front door of the first house they lived in on St. Clair Ave. in Sheboygan. The house on St. Clair Ave. was certainly unique unlike most houses built today. Gottlieb and Clementine Bauer lived in the original part of the house. Zeaman and Edna Dalhaimer lived in the upstairs portion of the original house after their marriage. Clementine added separate living quarters to the house so all her children's families could live there. My parents lived with Gottlieb and Clementine for a few weeks until the new addition on the house was built. On January 1, 1950, Gottlieb and Clementine moved into the new addition. My parents stayed in the first floor of the original house. Fred and Ruth Bauer moved into the 2nd floor addition. Each living quarter had its individual entrance.

Desserts

Above: Doris in her domain cooking in the kitchen on North 20th Street in Sheboygan, Wisconsin.

Left: Doris, at 78 years of age, still active and helping me in my kitchen in Chandler, Arizona.

Grebel

(Pronounced Greb el rhymes with rebel)

This dessert goes well any time of year. A Thalheimer tradition was to have this treat on Fat Tuesday, the day before Ash Wednesday prior to the start of Lent. Use a deep fryer if you have one. Otherwise, fry grebel in oil in the deepest pan you own. Use long utensils to place and remove grebel from oil.

Ingredients:

2 eggs	3 teaspoons water
8 oz. sour cream	2-¾ cups flour
1 teaspoon salt	¼ teaspoon baking powder
1 teaspoon sugar	6 cups vegetable oil
¼ teaspoon baking soda	Powdered sugar

Beat eggs in large bowl. Add sour cream, salt, and sugar. Put ¼ teaspoon baking soda in empty sour cream carton or a small bowl. Add 3 teaspoons of water to the container and mix.

Add the ingredients from the carton to the bowl with the sour cream, salt, and sugar. Add flour and baking powder and mix. Knead dough on cutting board with floured hands.

When dough is set, place dough and a drop of vegetable oil in a sealable bowl. Place wax paper over dough. Cover and seal the entire bowl tightly. Refrigerate overnight.

Next day, heat 6 cups of vegetable oil in an 8 qt. kettle or the largest, deepest kettle you own. Take dough out of the bowl and cut dough in half. Use rolling pin to roll out dough to approximately ¼ inch thick on cutting board. Cut the dough into one inch by three-inch rectangular strips.

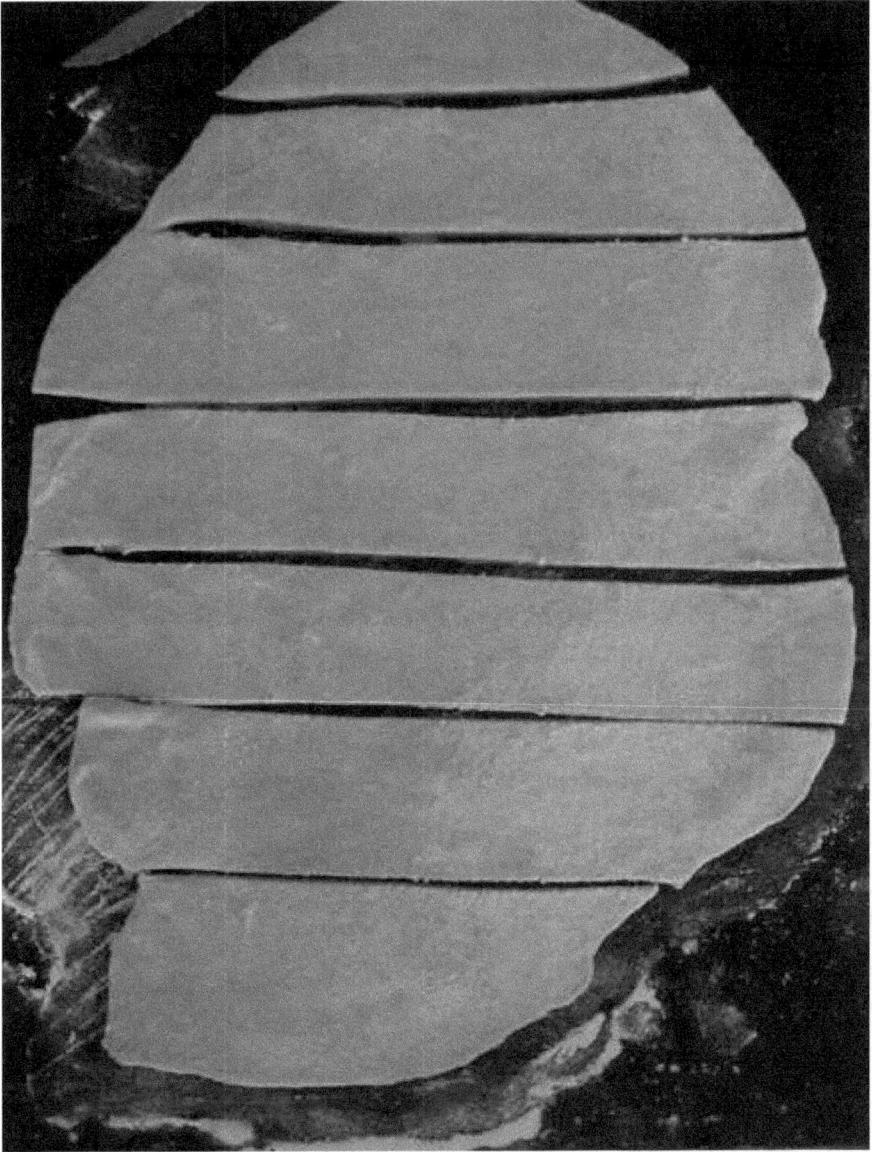

Rolled out dough cut into long strips. See the following page for creating the one inch by three-inch rectangular strips.

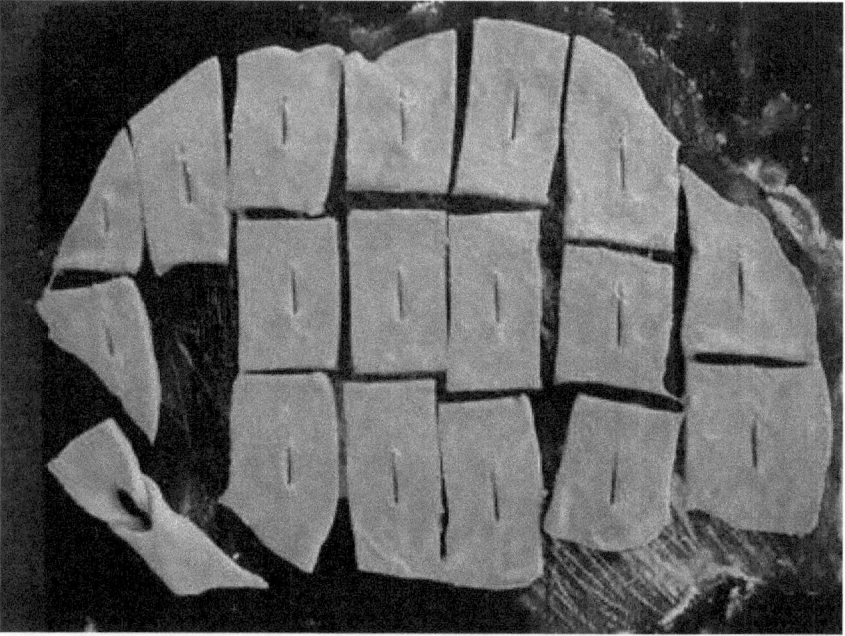

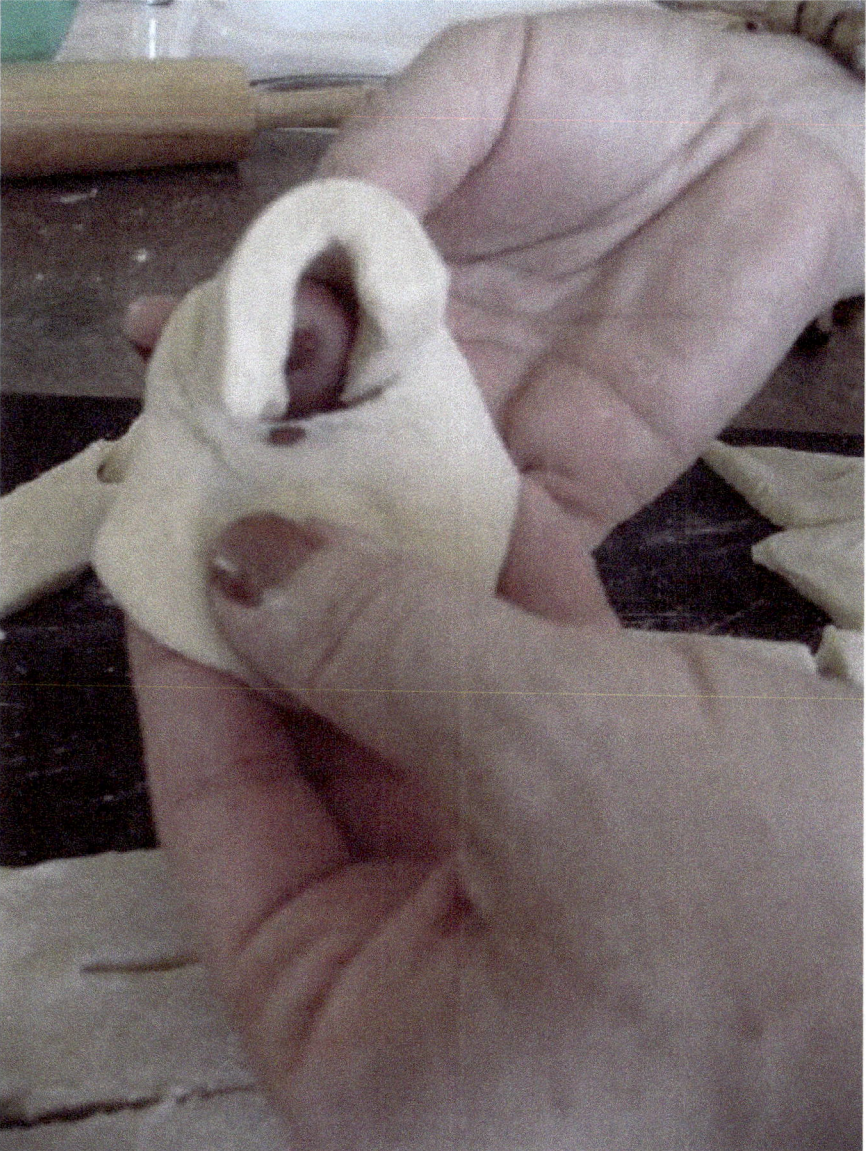

In the center of the strips, make a 1-½ inch slit. Hold one of the strips as shown in the picture pg. 62 and stretch the grebel slightly. Pull one end of the strip through the slit to create a twist.

The twisted dough called Grebel is ready for frying

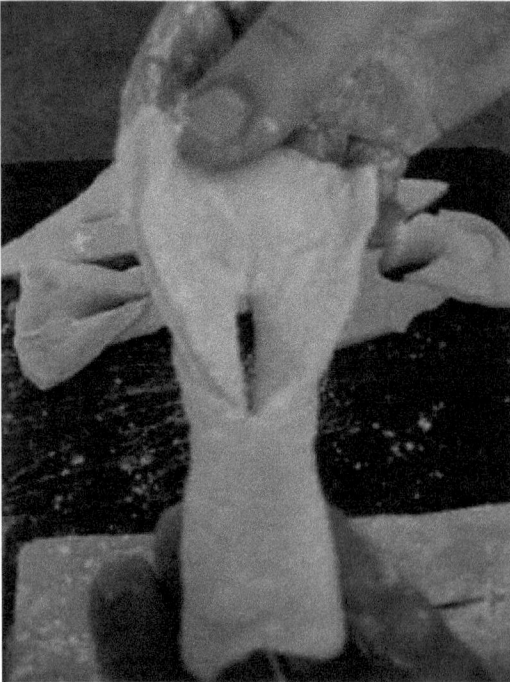

The perfect twist. Place twisted strips of dough in hot oil. Put only two or three grebel into the oil at a time

Heat grebel until it is golden brown on both sides. Remove from oil with long tongs and set on paper towel to dry.

Sprinkle each piece of grebel with powdered sugar. Use a handheld strainer filled with a couple tablespoons of powdered sugar and press the sugar with a spoon through the strainer onto the grebel.

*Eat as soon as possible following preparation
because grebel tastes great warm.*

Modern, healthy alternatives for Grebel:

* Use whole-wheat flour or Hodgson Mill all-purpose unbleached naturally white flour. Visit their web site at http://www.hodgsonmill.com/.
* Use organic, cage free eggs, eggbeaters, or egg replacers
* Use Smart Balance instead of butter

Beverage Recommendation:

A hot cup of your favorite brew of coffee or a glass of milk makes a great combination with grebel.

Butterhorns

This treat was a favorite of my mother's neighbors on 20th St. in Sheboygan, Wisconsin and in Klamath Falls, Oregon. Ach ya, butterhorns! A wonderful dessert or a fabulous breakfast treat. My nephew Steve makes a point to ask my mother, "Grandma, did you make butterhorns?" every time he visits. It makes an ideal schneck to serve during the holidays. Since it takes two days to make, I like to make this treat over the weekend.

Introducing German-Russian cooking to new family members was always an adventure. There are some meals we always believed that you had to "grow up on" to enjoy, however butterhorns are not one of them. When my niece, Christina Gamache married Chris Martin, Chris expressed a great deal of interest in making the German-Russian meals. He first made Ra Mauldasha on his own and subsequently asked my mother for her butterhorns recipe. Since it was only half written in my mother's recipe box, my mother was not comfortable handing it over without directions or explanation. So, Mom and I used my interpretation of her recipe and made a batch over Super Bowl weekend. Here is the best-written version of the recipe we have ever created, and it is dedicated to Chris and Christina. We hope you enjoy!

Making butterhorns with children is an excellent and memorable experience. If your children or grandchildren are learning geometry or you just enjoy playing together, this is a fantastic recipe everyone will enjoy. First, the dough is nearly the consistency of play dough. Shaping and rolling the dough is truly therapeutic after a rough week at work or school. Second, geometry and numbers play a big part. Besides measuring amounts, there are plenty of geometric designs from the rectangular cookie sheet, to the circular shape of the dough as it is rolled out, to the triangular shapes of the wedges to the crescent shape of the rolled butterhorn. Dare I mention fractions? My mother is completely mathematical about how many cookie sheets are used and how many butterhorns go on each sheet. Have fun playing with the numbers!

Ingredients:

4 cups flour (plus 1 cup for rolling out the dough)

1 cup melted butter (1/2 lb.)

¼ cup sugar 3 egg yolks, well beaten

¾ teaspoon salt 1 cup milk

1 pkg. dry yeast dissolved in 3 tablespoons water & a little sugar

1 tablespoon butter

For topping the rolled dough:

1 teaspoon cinnamon 3 teaspoons sugar

Mix the flour, sugar, salt, and butter in a large bowl. Add egg yolks, milk, and dry yeast mixture. Mix well with spoon and then knead with hands on floured board to make a smooth dough. Cover and refrigerate overnight.

The next day, melt 1 tablespoon butter. Mix 1 teaspoon cinnamon and 3 teaspoons sugar. Set aside.

Note the cinnamon and sugar mixture in the bowl above. While butter is melting, the dough is cut in 5 portions.

Cut the dough into 5 even portions. Select one part and flatten with your floured hands. Continue to thin the dough on floured surface with floured rolling pin until approximately a ¼ inch thick. Roll the dough into the shape of a round piecrust approximately 14 inches in diameter.

Brush the top of the rolled dough with approximately a fifth of the melted butter, and then sprinkle with cinnamon and sugar on it. Cut into 8 wedges.

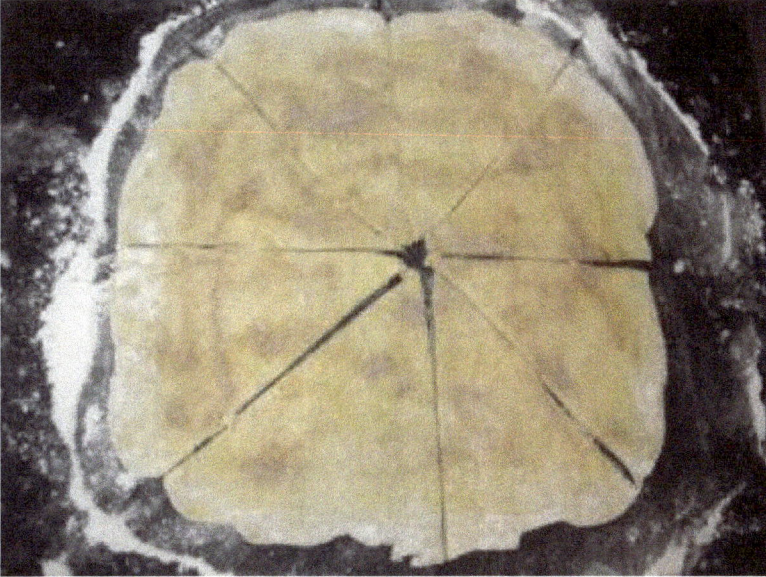

Roll up each piece from the outside edge of circle into a crescent shaped roll. Place rolled butterhorns on greased cookie sheet (traditionally the cookie sheet was ungreased, but I prefer a light spray of canola or olive oil to prevent sticking). Repeat this process with the remaining four portions.

Rolling the butterhorn from the outside edge

Brush melted butter on top of each rolled butterhorn and let the butterhorns rise in a warm place for 2 hrs. When my mother is at my sister Joan's house, she likes to set the butterhorns near the fireplace to rise. Another option is to pre-heat your oven, place the cookie sheets filled with butterhorns on the stovetop, and leave the oven door slightly ajar for 30 minutes. After 30 minutes, turn oven off, but leave door ajar. You can repeat heating the oven again after 1 hour.

Butterhorns rising for 2 hours.

Butterhorns on parade

After letting the butterhorns rise, bake at 375 ° F. for 15-20 minutes. Let cool and frost if desired. This recipe makes 40 butterhorns. Try to eat only one! Freezes well for at least 2 months.

FROSTING:
1 ½ -2 cups powdered sugar
2 tablespoons butter
3 tablespoons milk; add to gain desired consistency

Modern, healthy alternatives for Butterhorns:
- Use whole wheat flour, organic flour, or all-purpose unbleached naturally white flour
- Use soy milk instead of regular milk
- Use organic, cage free eggs, eggbeaters, or egg replacers

Beverage Recommendation:
Your favorite coffee flavor compliments butterhorns whether you eat it for breakfast, snack, or dessert. Try it with a shot of Cointreau!

KUCHEN
(Pronounced Koo ken or koo gen)

Besides the delicious taste of food, one of the greatest joys of cooking among generations is the memories shared and the memories created. Kuchen is a wonderful example of how memories pass from generation to generation.

My grandmother, Clementine, baked kuchen. It was one of the few recipes not recorded by my mother. Meals, family, and other regular life events just prevented them from finding the time. My mother discovered this recipe for kuchen and used it successfully for over fifty years. Kuchen makes a great dessert or morning coffee cake for breakfast.

My favorite memory of my mother making kuchen involves "flat grebel." "Flat grebel" was made from a small portion of the kuchen dough. Four "flat grebel" pieces were fried in oil each time my mother made kuchen. As a child, I always received this treat first, most likely because I was the youngest and was the one normally at home when she made it. I felt very special and saw this delight as exclusively for me. The "flat grebel" recipe was a tradition German-Russian cooks used when making dough. My mother only used this kuchen dough to create 'flat grebel."

What valuable memories will you share or create with your next cooking session?

Kuchen Ingredients:

1 cup lukewarm milk	¼ cup soft shortening
¼ cup sugar	1 cup raisins, optional
1 teaspoon salt	3 ½ to 3 ¾ cups flour
1 pkg. dry yeast	1 tablespoon vegetable oil
1 egg	Jam

Crumb topping:

2/3 cup sugar	2/3 cup Flour
2 teaspoons cinnamon	6 tablespoons butter
1 cup chopped nuts, optional	

Mix milk, sugar, and salt. Crumble the dry yeast into the mix and stir until it is dissolved. Add the egg and shortening. While we never added the raisins to our kuchen, it is certainly a healthy addition if you desire.

Slowly add the flour to the mix. Originally the recipe called for mixing by hand. Using a mixer works beautifully unless you need and are prepared for an arm workout. I opt for the mixer. Add a bit extra flour until dough is easy to handle.

Turn dough onto lightly floured board; knead until smooth and elastic. Place a little oil in a bowl. Set the dough on top of the oil for a moment. Then, turn the dough upside down so the greased side is on the top. Cover with damp cloth and set to rise at room temperature approximately 2 hours until indentation remains when two fingers are pressed deeply into dough. The dough will double in bulk. I always set the timer for 2 hours in case I become pre-occupied with other tasks.

Knead dough again by punching and rounding over and set to rise again for about 45 minutes. Repeat the kneading, set dough on board and cover with bowl or cloth for 15 minutes.

Prepare the Crumb Topping Recipe by mixing 2/3 cup sugar, 2/3 cup flour, and 2 teaspoons cinnamon. Blend in with 6 tablespoons of butter until crumbly. Stir in 1 cup chopped nuts if desired.

If you are making the flat grebel, slice a small part of the dough approximately one inch by four inches long. Set this small piece aside. Divide the large dough in half and pat each half into a greased round layer 9 x 1 1/2-inch pan. Press Crumb Topping into top of dough. Cover and let rise until an impression remains when dough is touched lightly with finger, approximately 25 to 35 minutes.

Bake 25 to 30 minutes in preheated 400° F. oven. Let cool. Sprinkle with sugar and spread strawberry jam over the top. You could use any flavor of jam you like. In our home, just do not expect my mother to eat anything other than strawberry jam.

The benefit of making kuchen is the creation of two desserts for one baking session. The photo shows the kuchen before adding strawberry jam.

Kuchen with strawberry jam

This plate belonged to Clementine Herrmann Thalheimer Bauer who gave it to my mother Doris Herzog Dalhaimer who gave it to me. On the back of the plate it reads: "The Harker Pottery Co. Quality Since 1840." See Appendix B for more details.

Modern, healthy alternatives for Kuchen:

- Use whole-wheat flour, organic flour, or all-purpose unbleached naturally white flour
- Use soy milk
- Use organic, cage free eggs, eggbeaters, or egg replacers

Beverage Recommendation:

Brew your favorite cup of coffee and enjoy.

Flat Grebel
(Pronounced Flat greb el rhymes with rebel)

Flat grebel is served on a small plate with sugar on the side.

Take the small piece of dough, which was set aside earlier and cut into four pieces. Stretch each piece out into a round circular shape. Place about a ¼ inch of oil into a frying pan and heat. When oil is hot, place the four pieces into the oil   Let grebel brown and then flip each piece to brown the other side. Cool the flat grebel on plate or paper towel. Serve to someone special on a small plate with a dusting of sugar for dipping.

Above: My sister Joan and I sitting on the small fence in front of Grandma Bauer's house. Right: My Dad and I at the Snafu Club. I stood still long enough for the picture to be taken on July 4, 1961. I am wearing my "U.S. Flag" shirt.

PINK PEPPERMINT COOKIES

These cookies have always been my favorite. I remember as a child being delighted when we visited my grandmother on St. Clair Ave. after she had baked these cookies. My grandmother made these cookies at any time of year, but certainly there would be plenty on Christmas Eve. My grandmother set out a smorgasbord of food for all her family and friends, which included the members of the Snafu Club. The Snafu Club was a softball organization and clubhouse, which my Dad and his brothers established in my grandmother's

garage. "Ma" Bauer, as she was affectionately known, was visited by players and friends on Christmas Eve. They enjoyed her great cooking. I knew the cookies would be there on Christmas Eve.

The Snafu clubhouse was no ordinary garage. It was designed as a place for members to relax after softball games, but it was a child's delight for my sister and me because there was a jukebox. Remember, this was the early 1960's and MTV was decades into the future. We listened to the latest hits and polkas on 45 records. Our favorite polka was "Just Because," by Frankie Yankovic. Joan and I danced and moved and probably did nothing that resembled a polka. We enjoyed every minute of it. I cannot remember what I ate for lunch yesterday, yet I can still remember the words to "Just Because." We also listened to the song "Wooden Heart" by Joe McDowell. My Dad's hobby was woodworking so each of his daughters received a wooden heart with our name on it.

So, these cookies are very special to me and evoke many memories. Originally, the recipe called for baking ammonia. Since the early 1990's, my mother has not been able to find this ingredient. It always sounded very strange to me to eat anything with ammonia as an ingredient; however, it never killed us. For fifteen years, we did not make the cookies because we could not find baking ammonia. In December of 2005, I searched the Internet for baking ammonia and discovered it now cost approximately $2.77 per ounce. I also found a homemade replacement using the 1 ½ teaspoons baking ammonia with 1 ½ teaspoons baking powder and 1 ½ teaspoon baking soda. We were extremely pleased with the results. Try it!

For more details on baking ammonia, see Appendix D. While the original recipe calls for 4 cups of flour, I have increased it to 5 cups to create more pliable dough with which it is easier to work. Add plenty of flour to the dough as you roll it out.

Ingredients:

1 cup vegetable or corn oil	4 cups flour
1 cup milk	2 teaspoons baking powder
2 eggs	1 ½ teaspoons baking ammonia*
1 cup white sugar	1 teaspoon peppermint drops
Pinch of salt	Red or green sugar, optional
	Red food coloring

*Replace baking ammonia with 1 ½ teaspoons baking powder and 1 ½ teaspoons baking soda if necessary

Pre-heat oven to 350° F. Grease cookies sheets with oil and set aside. Heat one cup oil and one cup milk in 2 qt. saucepan on stovetop. Beat 2 eggs in large bowl. Add 1 cup white sugar, heated oil, milk, and a pinch of salt to eggs. Mix in flour, baking powder and baking ammonia* (or substitute).

When mixed, add peppermint drops and sprinkle in red sugar and drops of red food coloring until color is a perfect pink. If anyone in your family is allergic to red dye, green sugar can be substituted for the red sugar. If either sugar or food coloring poses issues for anyone, just eliminate it because the white peppermint cookie also tastes great.

Mix ingredients and scoop large spoonfuls on floured surface. Use a rolling pin to roll out cookie dough. Add flour liberally if dough is too sticky to roll evenly to a thickness of approximately ½ inch.

Use a drinking glass to cut out the cookies from the dough. Turn glass upside down and place the top edge of it in flour until coated. Place the glass top side down on the dough to cut out round cookies.

Who needs a fancy round cookie cutter? Cutting out these cookies with a glass provides better control than a small cookie cutter.

Place cookies on oiled or greased cookie sheet. Sprinkle white, green or red sugar on top of each cookie. Mix and match sugars, as you like.

Lining up the cookies on the cookie sheet

Bake cookies for 12-15 minutes at 350° F.
This recipe makes about 47 cookies.

Modern, healthy alternatives for Pink Peppermint Cookies:

- Use all white or green sugar if anyone has allergies to red 40 dye or red food coloring
- Use safflower oil or canola oil in lieu of vegetable/corn oil
- Use whole-wheat flour, organic flour, or all-purpose unbleached naturally white flour
- Use organic, cage free eggs, eggbeaters, or egg replacers

Beverage Recommendation:

Milk, coffee, or both are wonderful options with the cookies

My Mom and Dad, both first generation Germans from Russia, celebrating their 50th Wedding Anniversary in 1999.

Butter Cookies

This recipe was used every year at Christmas, Valentine's Day, and Easter. The dough is perfect for cut out cookies of every shape from hearts and bells to Christmas trees and pumpkins. Round cookies cut from the top edge of the glass can be decorated like soccer balls for your soccer fanatic's birthday, baseballs for your favorite pitcher or tennis balls for the next Boris Becker. There are many cookie cutters shapes available from footballs to graduation caps. Have fun creating your own special occasions with unique shapes. These cookies are not only a delight to see, but also a great value compared to purchasing a dozen store made cookies. And think of the quality time you are spending with your family when you make your own cookies.

What do you do when the dough is so small you cannot cut out any shape? One of our traditions is to shape the last piece into a flattened, somewhat round shaped cookie. This cookie is always given to the youngest person, usually a child, to eat first.

INGREDIENTS:

1 cup butter	2 ¼ c. flour
1 cup granulated sugar	1 teaspoon cream of tartar
2 eggs	½ teaspoon baking soda
½ teaspoon vanilla	½ teaspoon lemon extract

Cream butter in mixer, add sugar and mix well. Add the eggs and continue mixing. Add the remaining ingredients and mix. Chill dough overnight.

Roll dough thin between a ¼ inch and ½ inch height on floured surface. Dip cookie cutter in flour and cut out in desired shapes. Place cut out cookie on greased cookie sheet.

Bake cookies at 375° F. for 10-12 minutes. After cooling, frost and/or decorate if desired. These cookies taste great whether plain or decorated.

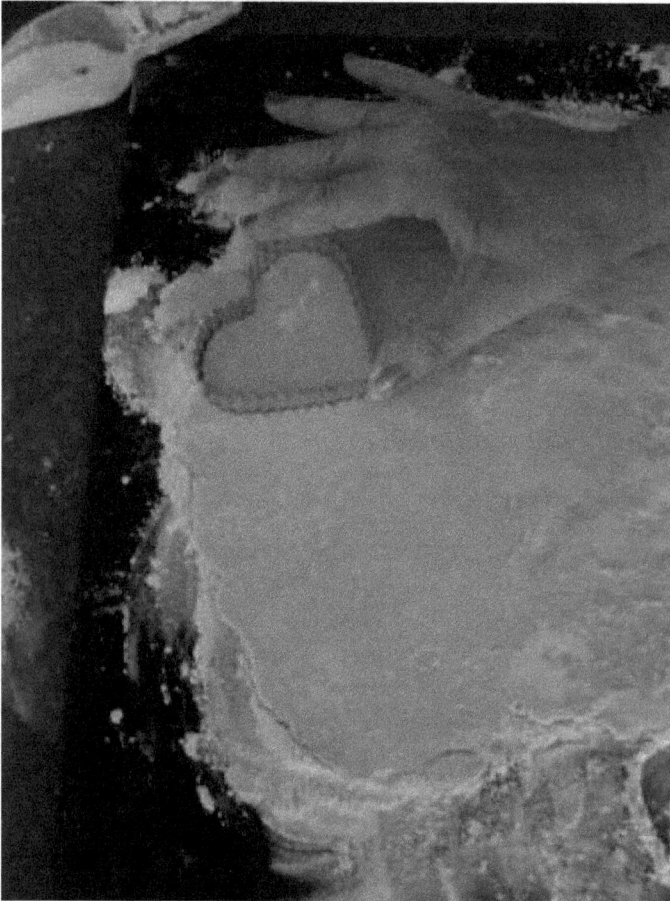

This beautiful lace edged heart cookie cutter was a gift from my daughter, Becky.

What a fun way to get ready for Valentine's Day! If you need help finding a specialty cookie cutter that your local stores do not stock, check out http://kitchengifts.com/ where you can find almost any design and place custom orders.

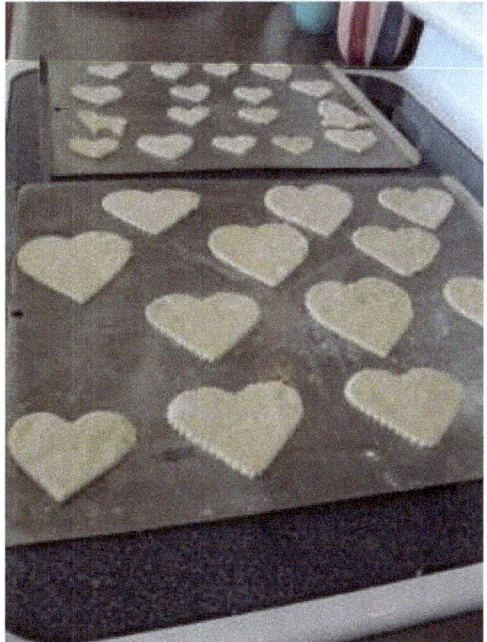

Frosting:

2 cups powdered sugar   2 tablespoons butter

3 tablespoons milk (if more moisture is needed, add a ½ tablespoon at a time)

Decorate with colored sugars, sprinkles, chocolate, or butterscotch chips, non-pareils, or whatever you fancy.

Modern, healthy alternatives for Butter Cookies:

- Use miniature cookie cutters for smaller cookies
- Use soy milk in place of regular milk
- Use Smart Balance instead of regular butter
- Use all-purpose unbleached naturally white flour or whole-wheat flour
- Use organic, cage free eggs, eggbeaters, or egg replacers

Beverage Recommendation:

A cool, tall glass of milk or a steaming, hot cup of coffee works well with these cookies.

Family Genealogy Update

Since the first printing of this book, I have successfully traced my family lines further back than I imagined possible. All four of my grandparents were born in villages in Russia. I traced back each line to the original settlers and their Germanic origins.

Wladimir's book the Herrmans tracks the family wider than the single line I researched and is the best guide for descendants of Nikolaus Herrmann. The Dalhaimers, originally listed as Thalheimer, Dahlheimer or other various spellings originated from Ansbach before Christopher Thalheimer moved his family to Mariental.

Jakob Herzog and his family from Kurpfalz originally settled in Balzer. His son, Leonard, moved to Reinwald prior to the 1798 census. J. Conrad Reimer of Württemberg died in Denmark while awaiting passage to Russia, however his wife and son, Konrad, continued the journey to become founding settlers of Reinwald. Descendants of J. Conrad Reimer have traveled around the world, and many of these descendants are in the province of Entre Rios, primarily Protestante, in Argentina.

Obviously, the expanded research would require many more pages than what is available in this book. My research continues to be a work in progress. Many of the family stories and research have been chronicled at http://valuemeals.blogspot.com/. I continue to learn and record more about my heritage every day.

If anyone shares my family lines, please contact me directly at anna@bart4.com so we can compare and learn about our heritage and family history together. Also, please check out two of my sites on Facebook: *Descendants of Reinwald, Russia* and *Descendants of Rosenfeld am Nachoi. Russia.* My cousin, Haydee Erbes Reimer, also has a wonderful site entitled *Descendientes de Heinrich Gottlieb Reimer* which covers the Reimer family in Argentina.

Best of luck to you in your research and cooking.

Thalheimer Family Bible

Die

Heilige Schrift

Alten und Neuen Testamentes.

Aus der Vulgata übersetzt von

Dr. Joseph Franz von Allioli.

Illustrirte Volksausgabe,

enthaltend den

vom apostolischen Stuhle approbirten vollständigen Text

mit einer auf 890 beigegebenen Bildern...

Mit Approbation des hochwürdigsten bischöflichen Ordinariates Augsburg.

Nebst dem

Katholischen Bibel-Wörterbuch

von

Augustin Calmet.

Neu bearbeitet von

Jahr. B. Raos, Pastor der St. Alphonsus Kirche, Philadelphia.

Mit besonderer Befürwortung

Des Hochwürdigsten Herrn James F. Wood, D.D

Erzbischof von Philadelphia.

er vom ewigen Vater auserwählten Tochter,

Der Gebärerin
des eingefleischten Wortes,

Der Braut des heiligen Geistes,

Dem erkorenen Liebling des allerheiligsten

DREIFALTIGKEIT,

Der Herrin der Engel, Der Beschützerin der Menschen,

Der Fürsprecherin der Sünder,
Der Zuflucht aller Bedrängten,
Der Königin
des Himmels und der Erde,

Die voll der Gnaden, gesegnet unter den Weibern,

Von jeder Makel der Erbsünde frei,

Als die Mutter des neuen Lebens den Namen der unglücklichen
Heva in einen Namen des Segens und der Wonne umschuf,

Mutter, und allezeit, vor, in, und nach der Geburt Jungfrau,

Die als die Morgenröthe heraufstieg,

um für dir, so in Finsterniß und Todesschatten sassen, du

Sonne der Gerechtigkeit
in den Erd-Kreis einzuführen,

GER.

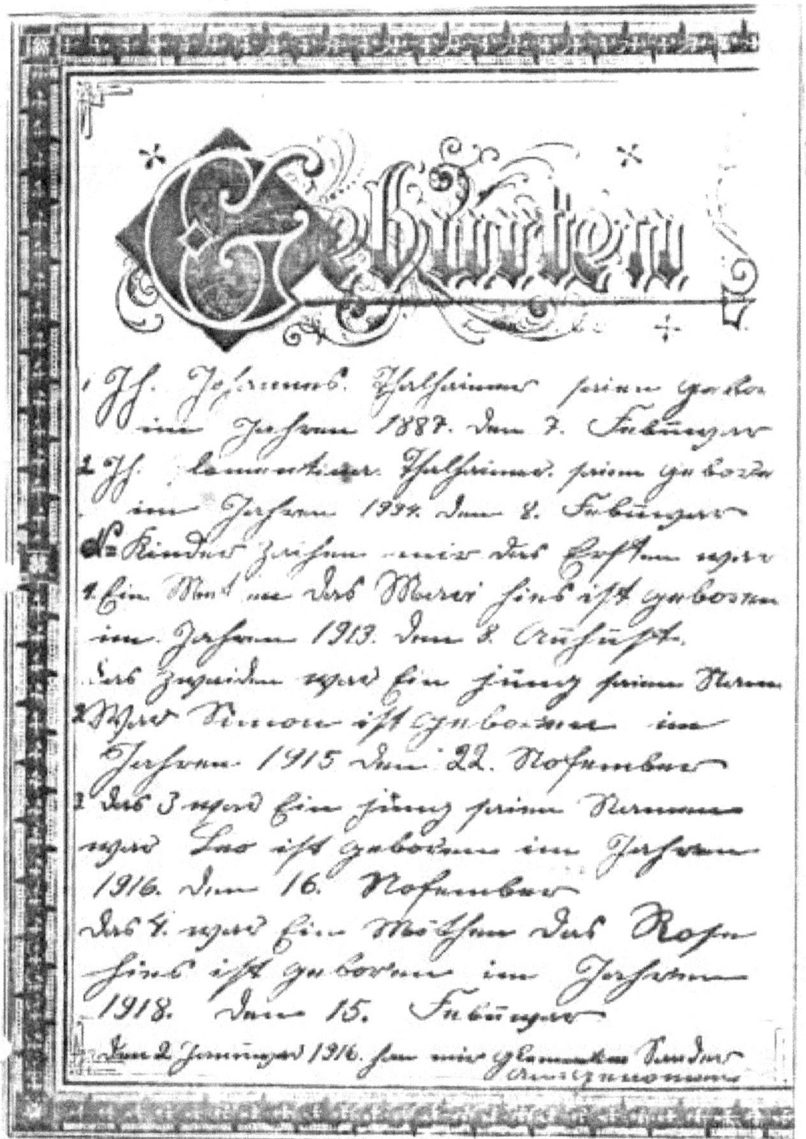

Geburten

(handwritten German entries in Kurrent script, largely illegible)

1. ... im Jahren 1887. Den 7. Februar

2. ... im Jahren 1894. Den 8. Februar

... Kinder ...

1. Ein ... der Marie sind ist geboren im Jahren 1913. Den 8. August.

2. ... ist geboren im Jahren 1915 Den 22. November

3. ... ist geboren im Jahren 1916. Den 16. November

4. ... der Rosa sind ist geboren im Jahren 1918. Den 15. Februar

Den 2. Januar 1916 ...

Pathen

Das 5. war ein Junge seinem Namen ist Simon ... ist geboren im Jahre 1920. Den 25. Mai ...

Das 6. war ein Junge seinem Namen ist Johann ... ist geboren im Jahre 1923. Den 25. ...

Das 7. war ein Junge seinem Namen ist Jakob ... ist geboren im Jahre 1925. Den 12. August.

Todesfälle

1. Marri – Thelfrimms ist gestorben im ... im 1913 ... 18. August

2. Simon Thelfrimms ist gestorben im Jahren 1915. Im 30. November

3. ... Thelfrimms ist gestorben im Jahren 1916. Im 16. November

4. Rosa Thelfrimms ist gestorben im Jahren 19.. den 12. November

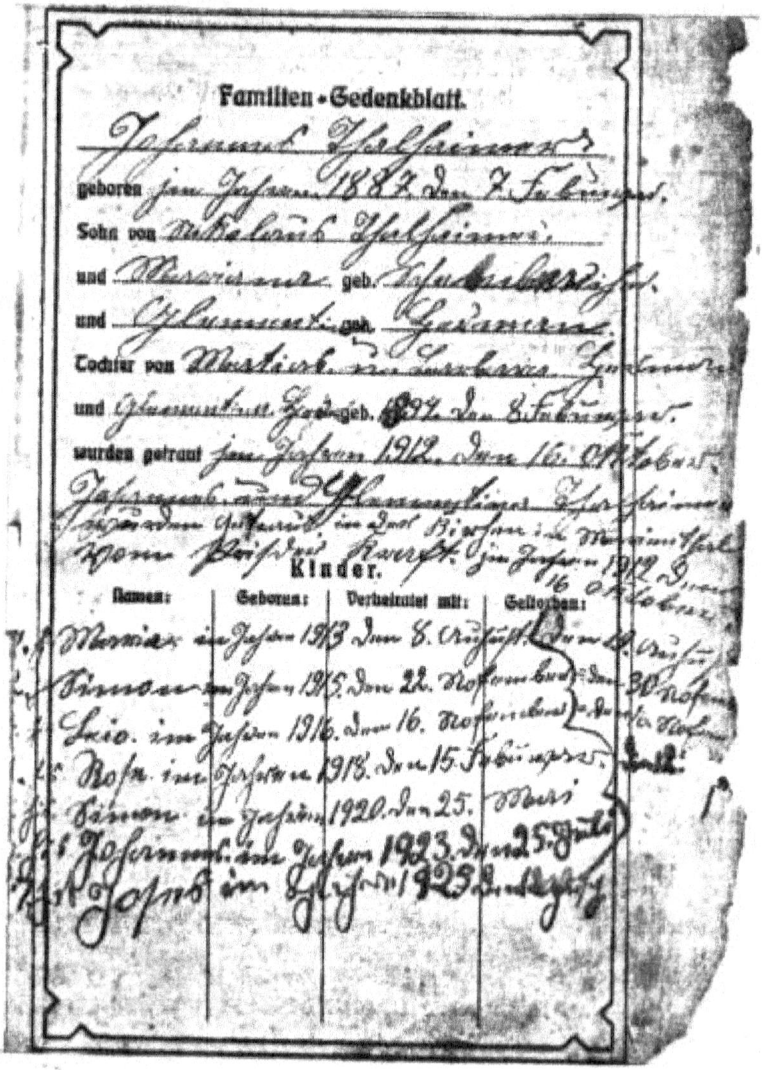

Appendix A

Mineral Water and Details re: Living in Sheboygan,

Wisconsin

In 1907, St. Peter Claver Church 's cornerstone was laid, and typhoid fever struck the city, the water works was blamed for polluted water. http://en.wikipedia.org/wiki/Sheboygan,_Wisconsin

Fountain Park 1000 Block, Eighth Street, Sheboygan, WI 53082, 920-459-3444, *Beautiful park featuring mineral fountains that are known for their supposed healing qualities. This park is also the home of the Civil War Memorial and to the Bandshell, the site of music concerts on Wednesday and Friday evenings during the summer.* For the purpose of obtaining a permanent water supply, the city of Sheboygan determined, in the spring of 1875, to bore an artesian well in the park. The contract was let to John Dobyns, who completed it to the depth of 1,475 feet in October following. An abundant supply of water was found at this depth, with a pressure of 52-1/2 pounds to the square inch, sufficient to raise a column 114 feet above the surface of the ground. The well cost the city about $5,000. A tasteful house, octagon in shape and surmounted by a bronze statue of Hebe, was erected at a cost of $1,600, and a large and handsome fountain in the center of the park, at a further outlay of $700 more. The water is richly impregnated with mineral salts, possessing medicinal value, as shown by the following analysis made by Prof. C. F. Chandler, Ph. D., of the Columbia College School of Mines, New York:

Chloride of Sodium	306.9436.
Chloride of Potassium	14.4822.
Chloride of Lithium	0.1062.
Chloride of Magnesium	54.9139.
Chloride of Calcium	27.8225.
Bromide of Sodium	0.1873.
Iodide of Sodium	Trace.

Sulphate of Lime	169.8277.
Sulphate of Baryia	Trace.
Bi carbonate of Lime	13.6585.
Bi carbonate of Iron	0.5944.
Bi carbonate of Manganese	0.1742.
Phosphate of Lime	0.0383.
Biborate of Soda	Trace.
Alumina	0.1283.
Silica	0.4665.
Organic Matter	Trace.
Total	588.2536.
Density	1.0093.

The medical effect of the water seems to be laxative, diuretic, and tonic. Physicians recommend its use for dyspepsia, rheumatism, faulty action of the liver and functional derangement of the kidneys and bowels. The water is very saline to the taste; but becomes grateful frequent use. Its value in the bath is undoubted. It is put up for shipment, under a lease from the city, by the Sheboygan Mineral Water Company, composed of E. R Richards, H. H. Kuentz and E. W. Koch. The water is put up in its natural state in lined kegs or barrels, and also is artificially charged with carbonic acid gas, giving it the healthful sparkle of seltzer, and put up in quart bottles and stone jugs The park and well are in charge of a Board of Commissioners, consisting of Mayor William H. Seaman, Chairman; Frank Geele, Conrad Krez, Christian Fricke and Gustav Mitwede. Col. Kres, who labored industriously to secure the digging of the well, is Clerk of the Board.
http://freepages.genealogy.rootsweb.com/~sheboygan/his13.htm

Appendix B
Harker Pottery Co.

A search of the internet uncovers this information about Harker Pottery Co. from http://www.mygrannysatticantiques.com/html/porcelain_pottery_chi na_marks_1.htm

The Harker Pottery Co. - East Liverpool, OH and Chester, WV - 1840 to 1972. The Harker Pottery Co. was one of the longest producing potteries in the US. It was established in 1840 in East Liverpool, OH, and later moved its facilities to Chester, WV in 1931. The Harker Pottery was sold to the Jeanette Glass Co. in 1969 but did not last long and closed its doors shortly afterward in 1972. Harker Pottery has a very interesting history and I suggest Lois Lehner's Encyclopedia of US Marks if you are interested in reading all of it.

One Harker mark that is seen quite often is the bow and arrow with the words "semi porcelain" and H.P.CO. Sometimes the initials are in script and can be above or below the graphic. Harker produced several wares such as: Cameoware (1940's), Quaker Maid (1960's to close), Harkerware, Hotoven (1930's & 1940's), Bakerite (kitchen accessories), Whitechapel and several others. Most are marked with Harker or variations there of.

Appendix C

Background on Pickling Spice

From HTTP://WHATSCOOKINGAMERICA.NET/Q-A/PICKLINGSPICE.HTM

Canning recipes that use pickling spices are usually referring to preparing and canning (foods preserved in bottles) anything that is pickled, like dill pickles, sour pickles, and sweet pickles. Some vegetables are also pickled and placed in jars for storing.

Pickling spice - pickling spice is most often used for canning pickles, but in some other dishes as well. The ingredients are cinnamon, mustard seed, bay leaves, allspice, dill seed, cloves, ginger, peppercorns, coriander, juniper berries, mace, and cardamom. For a hotter mix, add some crushed hot peppers. Makes about 1/4 cup.

2 cinnamon sticks, broken	1 tablespoon mustard seeds
2 teaspoons black peppercorns	1 teaspoon whole cloves
1 teaspoon whole allspice	1 teaspoon juniper berries
1 teaspoon crumbled whole mace	1 teaspoon dill seeds
4 dried bay leaves	1 small piece dried ginger

If you cannot find pickling spice and would rather buy it than make it, check out the following web site for pickling spice by Mrs. Wages for further details. http://www.canningpantry.com.
Pickling spice was available at Fry's (Kroger's) and Albertson's in March of 2006

Appendix D
Baking Ammonia

Notes regarding research on baking ammonia:
baker's ammonia = ammonium carbonate = carbonate of ammonia = baking ammonia = bicarbonate of ammonia = ammonium bicarbonate = powdered baking ammonia = triebsalz = hartshorn = salt of hartshorn = hirschhornsalz = hjorthornssalt = hartzhorn   Originally made from the ground antlers of reindeer, this is an ancestor of modern baking powder. Northern Europeans still use it because it makes their springerle and gingerbread cookies very light and crisp. Unfortunately, it can impart an unpleasant ammonia flavor, so it is best used in cookies and pastries that are small enough to allow the ammonia odor to dissipate while baking.
Look for it in German or Scandinavian markets, drug stores, baking supply stores, or a mail order catalogue. Do not confuse this with ordinary household ammonia, which is poisonous. *Varieties:* It comes either as lumps or powder. If it is not powdered, crush it into a very fine powder with a mortar and pestle or a rolling pin. *Substitutes (for 1 teaspoon of baker's ammonia):* 1 teaspoon BAKING POWDER (This is very similar but might not yield as light and crisp a product.) OR 1 teaspoon BAKING POWDER plus 1 teaspoon BAKING SODA

Check out these websites for more details:
http://www.foodsubs.com/Leaven.html#baker's%20ammonia
http://www.foodproductdesign.com/archive/2004/0904CC.html
www.kitchenproject.com/kpboard/
recipes/BakingAmmoniaCookies.htm

About the Author

Anna Dalhaimer Bartkowski is a second-generation American who is proud of her German-Russian ancestry. Her maternal grandparents were born in Reinwald and Rosenfeld am Nachoi. Her paternal grandparents were born in Mariental. The only grandparent still alive during Anna's lifetime was Clementine Thalheimer Bauer who was known as "Dina" or "Ma Bauer."

Anna has accumulated and saved much information regarding her family's history primarily due to her father's, Joseph John Dalhaimer, influence. His stories and knowledge of family events led her to re-discover the pleasure of traditional German-Russian cooking. Growing up in Sheboygan, Wisconsin with Bratwurst festivals, polkas and softball games kept much of the German-Russian community at the forefront of her life. Her mother, Doris, taught her to cook in the German-Russian tradition.

Always an avid reader and writer, Anna holds a bachelor's degree in Journalism from Marquette University. She currently resides in Arizona.

Write Cooking & Memory Notes here

Write Cooking & Memory Notes here

Write Cooking & Memory Notes here

Write Cooking & Memory Notes here

What are people saying about Value Meals on the Volga?

"Its's a lovely keepsake cookbook. Buy it!"
Thelma Mills, Mariental Village Coordinator,
American Historical Society of Germans from Russia

"Anna shows us how her relatives managed to elevate these simple ingredients (flour, eggs and dairy) into the delicious dishes that have become a part of her heritage."
Carolyn Niethammer, Author of *The Prickly Pear Cookbook* **and** *The New Southwest Cookbook*

"Valuable for anyone wanting to cook authentic German recipes on which we grew up. The directions are details and easy to follow. The photos of each step show exactly what to expect as food is prepared. The personal stories and pictures make fun and interesting German cookbook."
Theresa Scheaffer,
3rd Generation German from Russia

Be sure to visit www.blogspot.valuemeals.com for news on family history, cooking, and genealogical research by Anna Dalhaimer Bartkowski. Follow her on Facebook at www.facebook.com/annabartkowski or on twitter as annabartkowski.

www.ingramcontent.com/pod-product-compliance
Lightning Source LLC
Chambersburg PA
CBHW072158090426
42740CB00012B/2310